REPROGRAM
YOUR LIFE

Creative

Doug Wells

HOW TO CHANGE YOUR THOUGHTS
TO CHANGE YOUR LIFE

Reprogram Your Life

ISBN-13:   978-0-9837065-7-1

Reprogram Your Life

"How To Change Your Thoughts
To Change Your Life"

Doug Wells MS, LPC, CAMSII

DEDICATION

I would like to dedicate this book to my wife, children, family, friends and colleagues who have stood by me guiding me, directing me, encouraging me, and overall supporting me. Without them I would not be the person I am today.

Thank you all for your love and support.

This book is a powerful, energizing and life changing tool for growth and development. This information is not intended to be a substitute for medical care. If you are dealing with any sort of medical or emotional disorder or undergoing psychotherapy be sure to consult your physician or therapist and use this information under their supervision.

National Suicide Prevention Lifeline

Suicidepreventionlifeline.org

1-800-273-8255

24/7 free confidential support

Contents

What if you could write the story of your life?

What if you were in control of your destiny?

What if the
choices you
make today
affect the
outcomes of
your future?

The truth is, you can, you are in control of your destiny, you are writing the story of your life right now. The choices you make are directly related to the thoughts you have. That puts you in control, you have the ability to change the way you think, and when you change the way you think, you change your life.

The thoughts you are thinking right now are writing the story of your life. If you are not happy with the story, you can reprogram your thoughts to change the story and write it the way you want it to go.

Have you ever heard people say "It'll be ok, just think positive thoughts." There is actually a lot of good sound science behind the correlation of thoughts and feelings. Aaron Beck, one of the fathers of modern psychology taught us that we can change our mood or feelings by changing the way we think.

> Never underestimate your power to change yourself, and never overestimate your power to change others
>
> ~ Dr. Wayne Dyer ~

Have you ever tried to just think positively? Most of the time just thinking positive is easier said than done, but it is not impossible. There is a way to reprogram your life, you can learn how to change your life by changing the way you think. The reprogram your life paradigm not only concentrates on the cognitions (thoughts), but spiritually as well, for with God all things are possible (Mathew 19:26)

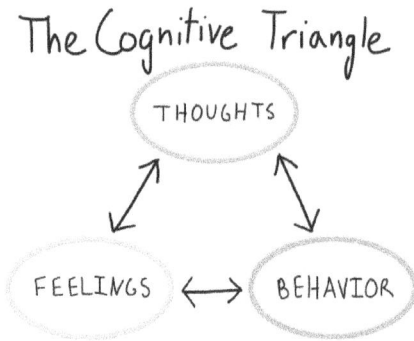

The Cognitive Triangle

THOUGHTS

FEELINGS ⟷ BEHAVIOR

Aaron Beck taught cognitive behavioral therapy, which is based on the idea that how we think (our cognitions), how we feel (our emotions), and how we act (our behaviors), all interact together. A shorter way of saying this is, **our thoughts determine our feelings which dictated our behaviors**. How this can manifest in our life is: Our negative and unrealistic thoughts can cause us distress, which results in problems.

When we suffer from psychological distress (Stress, Anxiety), the way in which we interpret situations becomes skewed, our thoughts become more dark, more negative, it is harder to see the positive in things, this can have a negative impact on the actions we take. Those negative thoughts foster the negative feelings, which create the negative behaviors. You see they are all connected. It is like this crazy triangle with each point having a direct effect on the others.

Unfortunately the negative things just seem to flow more easily. But when you put the energy into the positive points they can have just as real of an effect on the others. By changing any of the points we effectively change the other two points as well. When you are having happy positive thoughts, that effects the way you feel. These positive thoughts will generate happy feelings. When you are thinking positive and feeling happy your behaviors will be in alignment and others will notice. Do you see the connection? You can reprogram your behaviors and feelings by changing the thoughts you are having.

We interact with the world around us through our mental representation of the world. If our mental representations are inaccurate or our ways of reasoning are inadequate, then our emotions and behaviors may become disordered. Albert Ellis, yet another prominent figure form psychology's not so distant past, told us a way to deal with these irrational beliefs is to reframe the experience. Ellis teaches us to re-interpret our experience in a more realistic light. This helps us to develop more rational beliefs and healthy coping strategies.

Reframing is a very effective tool used by psychologists all around the world to help us change the way we see things. Our prepetition is not always as it seems. Remember when you ask two people about a particular event there is person one's version, person two's version and then there is the truth. Each of us sees things from our own angle. Change the angle and the thing we are seeing changes.

Many of our thoughts occur automatically, without us putting any effort into it at all. The thoughts just happen. In reality this is a good thing. By having automatic thoughts we don't have to work too hard to do daily or routine tasks such as getting up, getting dressed, eating breakfast, going to work and so on. When we first were learning to do each of these tasks it took effort and thought. We may have even failed several times and had to be shown by others how to do these tasks. However, as we perfected them and did them over and over they became easier and we did them without too much effort at all.

There is an old saying practice makes perfect, it is incorrect. The statement is more accurate as "practice make permanent". You see you can do something over and over again and never actually get it right or even close to perfect. What you will do is cement the process into your brain and whatever the task is and however you perform it, it will become permanent. When this happens the processing of the task is moved from your conscious mind into your unconscious or habitual mind.

Before you say, man these automatic thoughts are awesome, where can I get more of them, remember everything has it's opposite. Automatic thoughts can also be a bad thing, as many of these automatic thoughts become habitual and therefore we do not pay much attention to them. These habitual thoughts happen all the time and we don't even realize they are occurring. These habitual thoughts happen subconsciously, we get so used to the negative thoughts they just become a part of our normal thinking.

"You are the product of all the choices you have made in your life"

~ Dr. Wayne Dyer ~

Negative thought patterns can start from childhood onwards. Sometimes these mind viruses can be given to us by people who are trying to do good. People in our lives who love us and want the best for us. They themselves are ignorant of the harm they may be doing because they do not know what they do not know.

You see people go through life doing the best they can with the knowledge they have at the time. You and I are both guilty of this, just like everyone else in the world. That does not change the fact that **there is a better way of doing things.** It is simply a fact that we did not know, so we did the best with the knowledge we had at the time. It is kind of amazing how much power people can have over our lives at different times.

"When people are able to change their thinking, they can approach their daily lives and problems with much more energy and confidence."

~ Sally Connolly ~

For example, if you didn't receive much attention or praise from your parents or teachers at school, you might have thought "I'm useless, I'm not good enough". Over time you might come to believe these assumptions, until as an adult these negative thoughts become automatic. This way of thinking might then affect how you feel at work, school or in your general life. If your negative interpretation of situations goes unchallenged, then these patterns in your thoughts, feelings and behavior can become part of a continuous cycle.

Negative thought leads to negative thinking, identifying this is the first step toward letting it go. The following are the common types of negative thinking. There is overlap among them, but naming them makes it easier to remember them.

Types of Negative Thinking

- **All-or-Nothing Thinking**.

    "I have to do things perfectly, because anything less than perfect is a failure."

- **Disqualifying the Positives**.

    "Life feels like one disappointment after another."

- **Negative Self-Labeling**.

    "I feel like a failure. I'm flawed. If people knew the real me, they wouldn't like me."

- **Catastrophizing**.

    "If something is going to happen, it'll probably be the worst case scenario."

- **Mind Reading**.

    "I can tell people don't like me because of the way they behave."

- **Should Statements**.

    "People should be fair. If I'm nice to them, they should be nice back."

- **Excessive Need for Approval**.

    "I can only be happy if people like me. If someone is upset, it's probably my fault."

- **Disqualifying the Present**.

    "I'll relax later. But first I have to rush to finish this."

- **Dwelling on Pain**.

    "If I dwell on why I'm unhappy and think about what went wrong, maybe I'll feel better." Alternately, "If I worry enough about my problem, maybe I will feel better."

- **Life is a struggle**.

    "I don't think we are meant to be happy. I don't trust people who are happy. If something good happens in my life, I usually have to pay for it with something bad."

Consequences of Negative Thinking

Negative thinking is an obstacle to self-change.

Any change feels like a big deal.

You can't see the small steps, and you don't have the energy to take big steps, therefore you feel stuck.

All-or-nothing thinking is the most common type of negative thinking. This kind of thinking leads to anxiety because you think that any mistake is a failure, which may expose you to criticism or judgment. Therefore you don't give yourself permission to relax and let your guard down. All-or-nothing thinking can also lead to depression, because when you think you have to be perfect, you feel trapped by your own unrealistic standards. Feeling trapped has a high correlation to the onset of depression.

Finding Positive in your life

Cognitive behavioral therapy can help identify and challenge negative thinking patterns and behaviors. Cognitive behavioral therapy is a talking therapy which focuses on how your thoughts, beliefs and attitudes affect your behaviors and feelings. Through cognitive behavioral therapy you can learn coping skills to deal with difficult problems. Cognitive behavioral therapy is a combination of cognitive therapy, or the process of examining your thoughts, with behavioral therapy, or the process of examining the things you do.

The way we think about situations can affect the way we feel and behave. For example: if you perceive a situation in a negative way , you might experience negative emotions as a result. These negative feelings may lead you to behave in a certain way. Cognitive behavioral therapy is flexible and can be adapted to meet everyone's needs. Through cognitive behavioral therapy you can learn to identify what you need to change, and how to start that change. You can learn healthy coping skills and how to incorporate changes in your life.

Although this book is filled with some great information and techniques to help you make real change in your life, it is not meant to be a substitute for traditional therapy. If your problems seem too large to manage, and you feel you are struggling too much, contact a therapist in your area. I know there may be a stigma attached to "seeing in therapist", but don't let what you think others might think stop you from progressing.

Go to www.psychologytoday.com and find a therapist/counselor in your area. Take this book with you, working together you will be able to achieve your goals even faster. Ok, commercial over, I mean I am a therapist so I would be remiss in not taking the opportunity to plug the profession some. But really if you need extra help do not be afraid to ask.

POWER OF THOUGHT

Your thoughts control your behaviors. Everything you do starts as a thought. Some thoughts you are very much aware of, like which shirt you pick out to wear. Other thoughts you are not aware of, like putting one foot in front of another as you walk down the sidewalk. The thoughts you are not aware of are your unconscious thoughts or automatic thoughts. These thoughts have become habitual, because you have had them so many times. They are now thoughts you have without thinking about them, they just simply happen.

Thoughts are such an incredible thing. Thoughts bring everything to pass. Anytime anything has ever happened in the world it was first perceived by a thought. I mean think about it even God, when he made this beautiful world for us had a thought about it first. Thanks to technology we have come a long way in understanding the world around us. Scientists have discovered that every thought has a different electronic signature. This means that thought can be measured by their wave lengths, we can actually see our thoughts, or at least the wave patterns created by the electric circuitry of our brains.

Watch your thoughts, they become words,

Watch your words, they become actions,

Watch your actions, they become habits,

Watch your habits, they become character,

Watch your character, it becomes your destiny

Every one of us is capable of thinking in a positive way if we want to. Often times though, we default to negative thinking, and the idea we cannot do certain things. You see there are these ANTs running around in our brain. Not the 6 legged kind you find at a picnic, but rather Automatic Negative Thoughts (ANT).

"I don't believe in pessimism. If something doesn't come up the way you want, forge ahead. If you think it's going to rain, it will."

~ Clint Eastwood ~

These things can be tenacious. Just like the picnic ants who invade the peaceful event with our friends and loved ones, these ANTs invade the peacefulness of our mind. You know when you leave little bits of crumbs around and the picnic ant scout finds them, then he goes and tells his friends and they all show up. The same thing happens with ANTs. Once we get a few crumbs of negative thoughts in our mind the others tend to show up and bring friends. It all starts with just the smallest of thoughts, those thoughts may even be put there by other people without knowing they are starting a storm of fire ANTs (had to throw in a Texas reference).

Way too many people today grow up hearing that they cannot do what they want in life; that they cannot pursue a certain profession or task. They are told over and over again by people close to them things like "you'll never be able to do that." This meme grows inside you and you begin to believe it and you end up living up to just those statements. These statements from our family, friends, co-workers, neighbors, church leaders, become a part of us and start to define us. This creates a limited belief system that we begin to live by as we grow. This belief system is not about religion, it is about you, your attitude, and opinion about the world around you. It is about the beliefs you have about yourself.

For the average person you have heard "No, you can't" about 1,500 times before you are 18. In the same time period you have heard "yes, you can" about 500 times. This creates a very powerful belief system of " I can't". This meme has taken hold and you begin to live by these thoughts. Beliefs are many times stronger than desires. If you desire something like a new job or a new car it will not come to pass, because you believe "you can't". For most of us, we have things backwards, we believe that we feel or think a certain way because of the circumstances. But the truth is our thoughts are creating the

"Man is but the product of his thoughts –
What he thinks he becomes."

~ Mahatma Gandhi ~

circumstances in our life. If we learn to use this to our advantage, we can truly change our life by changing our thoughts. Your subconscious mind or habitual mind is where the deep-seated beliefs are stored. If you want to change the circumstances in your life and begin to start attracting to yourself that which you want, you must first learn to reprogram your life.

Don't obsess over your thoughts, rather simply become aware of them. There is great importance in becoming aware of your habitual thoughts and to learn to appropriately adjust your thoughts in order to maintain a more positive mental attitude. As you do this be cautious that you do not become obsessed with every thought that comes into your mind. This can be overwhelming and counter-productive. When you obsess over the negative thoughts you give them power. Remember what you think about you bring about. When you do this with the negative thoughts, you empower the saying "what you resist persists." Other than resisting you negative thoughts practice replacing them with more positive thoughts as they arise.

"Your thoughts create your life"

~ Louis Hay ~

Not all thoughts are created equal, the power of any particular thought is determined by how often you have that thought and by the strength of the feelings or emotions associated with it. It is as though feelings are the power horse behind the thought. The stronger the feelings the more power the thought has . A thought by itself is basically just an idea. When you associate a feeling with the thought you give the thought the power to change your life.

Whether you know it or not you have quite literally been creating the story of your life by influencing the situations and circumstances around you with your thoughts. **You can use the power of thought to change your life.** It is within your subconscious or habitual mind where your deep seated beliefs live. To change the circumstances and attract into your life that which you choose, you must first learn to reprogram your habitual mind by changing your thoughts.

When you start becoming more aware of your habitual thoughts it is very easy to begin to obsess over them. It is important that as you become more aware of these thoughts you appropriately adjust them so that you maintain an overall positive mental attitude. As you do this be careful not to become obsessed with every thought that enters your mind. What you resist you persist, so do not obsess over your unwanted negative thoughts, this only gives them power. Rather than resist the negative thoughts simply replace the negative ones with more positive thoughts as they arise.

A very effective technique to take the power away from the negative thoughts is to instantly replace these unwanted negative thoughts with an opposite, positive thought. For instance; if you

"Man becomes what he thinks about"

~ Morris E. Goodman ~

think to yourself, "I'm not good enough, I will never succeed." Mentally replace the thought with "I am good enough, and success comes easily to me."

By reprogramming the dominate negative thought you have on a regular basis with a positive thought, the other random negative thoughts will follow suit. On any given day a person has upwards of 70,000 thoughts. There is no way a person can control each one of the 70,000 thoughts, but you can control the more dominate habitual thoughts and bring them under control. As you change these dominate negative thoughts to more positive thoughts you will be changing your mental attitude. As your mental attitude becomes more positive, your random thoughts will fall in line and become more positive as well.

Once you become aware of the power of thought, you will have more power to be able to change your life. Look around you, everything you can see has come into existence because of thought. Thoughts become actions, and actions become things. Just as how Mr. Chair invented that soft comfortable sitting device, by coming up with the thought of a chair, then the thought became an action, which resulted in the physical chair being made. You to create the things in your life starting with the thoughts you have.

The things you think about expand into the world around you. As these thoughts expand similar things are attracted and show up in your life. An example of how this may happen would be: As you are watching a great movie titled *Rin Tin Tin*, you think to yourself, that is beautiful German Shepherd. Throughout the rest of the movie you fall in love with Rin Tin Tin. After the movie is over and you are walking home, you begin to notice German Shepherds everywhere. There is not any more German Shepherds than before you watched the movie. The German Shepherds did not magically appear. You simply have attracted them into your life by the thoughts you were having of the German Shepherd Rin Tin Tin, and the emotions you felt when you were having the thoughts, gave it the power to expand and attract similar things into your life.

The power which thought has is so amazing, you literally create the story of your life through the thoughts which you have. If you are not happy with the story so far, you can rewrite the story as you go and change how the story proceeds. Start with a simple first step. Begin to believe that you have the power to change your life.

"As you think, so shall you be."

There is no such thing in life as coincidences', everything happens for a reason. We may never really know the reason but there is always a reason none the less. Carl Yung called this the Law of Synchronicity.

Jung believed life was not a series of random events but rather an expression of a deeper order. This deeper order led to the insights that a person was both embedded in a universal wholeness and that the realization of this was more than just an intellectual exercise, but also had elements of a spiritual awakening. From the religious perspective, synchronicity shares similar characteristics of an "intervention of grace". Jung also believed that in a person's life, synchronicity served a role similar to that of dreams, with the purpose of shifting a person's egocentric conscious thinking to greater wholeness.

In his book Synchronicity Jung tells the following story as an example of a synchronistic event:

My example concerns a young woman patient who, in spite of efforts made on both sides, proved to be psychologically inaccessible. The difficulty lay in the fact that she always knew better about everything. Her excellent education had provided her with a weapon ideally suited to this purpose, namely a highly polished Cartesian rationalism with an impeccably "geometrical" idea of reality. After several fruitless attempts to sweeten her rationalism with a somewhat more human understanding, I had to confine myself to the hope that something unexpected and irrational would turn up, something that would burst the intellectual retort into which she had sealed herself. Well, I was sitting opposite her one day, with my back to the window, listening to her flow of rhetoric. She had an impressive dream the night before, in which someone had given her a golden scarab — a costly piece of jewelry. While she was still telling me this dream, I heard something behind me gently tapping on the window. I turned round and saw that it was a fairly large flying insect that was knocking against the window-pane from outside in the obvious effort to get into the dark room. This seemed to me very strange. I opened the window immediately and caught the insect in the air as it flew in. It was a scarab beetle, or common rose-chafer (Cetonia aurata), whose gold-green color most nearly resembles that of a golden scarab. I handed the beetle to my patient with the words, "Here is your scarab." This experience punctured the desired hole in her rationalism and broke the ice of her intellectual resistance. The treatment could now be continued with satisfactory results.

To phrase it simply, the things that happen in our lives which we have become accustom to calling coincidences', are in actuality Devine events which have been allowed to happen in a sequence which we do not understand in order for the Devine plan of Heaven to be carried out.

How we perceive things…

Have you ever noticed how some people seem to have the world in their hand, it doesn't matter what comes their way, they always seem happy? There is nothing special about this type of people. They are not any more blessed than you. The only difference is the way they look at things. Everybody looks at things differently. There really is not a right or wrong way to look at things. **It simply comes down to how we choose to view the world around us.**

Our world view is based on our experiences, it is influenced by others around us, it is how we choose to see things. The interpretations we place on the experiences we have each and every day. Every time we experience something we choose how we are going to look at it. What our perceptions to the event will be. Sometimes those

> When you change the way you look at things, the things you look at change
>
> ~ Dr. Wayne Dyer ~

choices are automatic, the response is habitual, a result of a meme we previously allowed ourselves to be conditioned to. Even these habitual or automatic perceptions were our choices originally. We have just made them so often they have become the natural way we look at things. They have become part of our personality. By understanding our perceptions, the way we look at things, is our choice, this allows us to have control. We have the ability to choose another way of looking at things. The interesting part of this is that when we change the way we look at things, the things we look at change.

Imagine if you were to take an experience you have had and change the way you perceived it. If you were to change your attitude toward that thing, if you were to completely change the way you look at it. Take for instance if you are having a bad day. We all have bad days. Days when nothing seems to go our way, when it seems the cards are stacked against us. When you are feeling yourself being beaten by the circumstances. Pause for a moment. Take a deep breath, maybe even go to a quiet place and close your eyes, just for a few moments. During this time make a conscious effort to think about the things you are thankful for. Think of the things that have or are going right. Even when everything seem to be going bad, that isn't truly the case, there are things that are going right. Occasionally you may have to think hard, but there is always positive things around you. Focus on those positive things. The things that are going right, the things you are grateful for. As you think of these things focus on the feelings associated with these positive experiences.

Now go back about your day. Remembering these positives. Let the things that are not going right take a back seat to the things that are going right. By making this choice your day will turn around and the positive energy will follow into your

"If you believe you can, or if you believe you cannot, either way you are correct."

~ Henry Ford ~

life and that bad day will become a better day, maybe even a good day.

Our perceptions shape our reality. Most of us live our lives by the way we view the world around us. The attitudes we adopt is a result of our world view. And that attitude is what makes our reality. Changing your behavior changes how you feel much more than thinking about your behavior does. Remember the triangle from before. When you change your behavior it has a direct effect on your thoughts and feelings. Learning to change our thoughts is how we learn to reprogram our lives.

ATTRACTION

You attract into your life what you are....

You may have heard of the law of attraction or "the Secret". The law of attraction has been described in many different ways over the years, plainly stated it is: Everything coming into your life is the result of what you have been attracting into your life. I have a certain take on the law of attraction which may slightly differ from that of others. My take on the law of attraction is you attract into your life those things that you are.

You live your life a specific way, your thoughts are aligned with the way you behave. Your life will line up with the way you are, the thoughts you have, the behaviors you do and the way you live. The law of attraction does not care if things are negative or positive, it is not bias to wants or don't wants. It works on the energy you are putting out. Through years of personal experience along with years of assisting others along their journey, I have come to realize the law of attraction is real. It is a natural law which through the complexities of synchronicity, Jesus aligns our lives.

What if God uses the laws so that we have more control over our lives? The apostle Paul stated that all things are ours whether the world or life or death or the present or the future, they are ours. God gave us agency to choose, the ability to make choices in our lives, even though He knows what would be best, He gave us the ability to choose right or wrong it is our choice. Through this agency is a way the law of attraction works in our lives.

Jesus showed us how the law of attraction works in our relationships with others: "Be ye therefore merciful, as your Father also is merciful. Judge not, and ye shall not be judged: condemn not, and ye shall not be condemned: forgive, and ye shall be forgiven: Give, and it shall be given unto you; good measure, pressed down, and shaken together, and running over, shall men give into your bosom. For with the same measure that ye mete withal it shall be measured to you again." Luke 6:36-38.

When you add redemptive grace through your faith in Christ you kick start the law of attraction into high gear. "Therefore I say unto you, What things soever ye desire, when ye pray, believe that ye receive them, and ye shall have them." Mark 11:24.

"However the law of attraction works, whatever goes on in our minds attracts the objects of our imagination to us, thereby creating a new real of our imaginations to itself. When we truly understand the law of attraction, it encourages us to be good stewards of our thoughts." (More to the Secret)

The secret to the law of attraction is God and his will always takes precedence over the law of attraction. We should seek first the kingdom of God and use this law to bless the lives of others. There is nothing wrong with using the law of attraction, but we should shift the bias for happiness away from the laws, our happiness needs to remain firmly rooted in one person, Jesus Christ and our love and trust in Him. The law of attraction is repeated throughout the scriptures. "Be not deceived; God is not mocked: for whatsoever a man soweth, that shall he also reap." Galatians 6:7

In the scriptures, the law of attraction is better known as the law of the harvest. The scriptures teach us of laws irrevocably decreed in Heaven. One of these laws is the law of the harvest. Simply put the law of the harvest says "you reap the rewards of that which you sow"

We can all agree it would be crazy for a farmer to expect corn to grow if he did not work the ground, prepare it properly, plant the corn seeds and provided the water. In order to receive the thing he wants, the corn, he must do his part of the work. The farmer has to have the desire for the corn harvest, and do all he can to prepare the ground, plant and nurture the seeds. Then after doing all he can and having faith in the natural law, he receives the reward of a bountiful corn harvest.

We all know there are times when the farmer does everything right and the harvest fails. Maybe a bug infestation or a drought comes and the fields don't produce a harvest. These are the things which remind us that God has a part in everything that happens. Just because we do everything the way we think we are supposed to, it doesn't mean it is in line with God's plan. God is in charge, we don't have to understand the reasoning or the plan, we only have to have faith and do our part. He will make up the difference. I might suggest that those times when we do what we think is right and they don't work out, this could be that our plan/thoughts are miss-aligned with God's plan. Through pray and study we can re-align ourselves with God. When our lives are in alignment with God amazing things happen.

The Lord has clearly charted a course for us to obtain his blessings. He is bound by his divine law to bless us for our righteousness. The overwhelming question in each age is why each generation must test his law, when the Lord's performance from generation to generation has been absolutely consistent.

"Be not deceived; God is not mocked: for whatsoever a man soweth, that shall he also reap. For he that soweth to his flesh shall of the flesh reap corruption; but he that soweth to the Spirit shall of the Spirit reap life everlasting. And let us not be weary in well doing; for in due season we shall reap." Gal. 6:7–9.

In this world of turmoil, as we look at what the harvest will be for our personal lives, these words of Bernard M. Baruch hold great meaning: "The only freedom man can ever have is the freedom to discipline himself. That is what we are fighting for, to maintain our right to self-discipline instead of having the discipline of slavery and tyranny thrust upon us by a conquering enemy."

Scholars often point to the great battles of history and indicate how the fate of the world is shaped by the outcome. Such battles were fought at Waterloo, Concord, Gettysburg, and Normandy. However, after careful analysis one must conclude that the great and determining battles are fought within the soul of man.

Each day of our own lives we are faced with similar decisions. These choices determine the ultimate course of our lives. It is the culmination of our day-to-day decisions and actions that determines whether we will reap a harvest of peace in this life and life eternal, or unhappiness.

"Then shall the King say unto them on his right hand, Come, ye blessed of my Father, inherit the kingdom prepared for you from the foundation of the world: For I was an hungered, and ye gave me meat: I was thirsty, and ye gave me drink: I was a stranger, and ye took me in: Naked, and ye clothed me: I was sick, and ye visited me: I was in prison, and ye came unto me. Then shall the righteous answer him, saying, Lord, when saw we thee an hungered, and fed thee? or thirsty, and gave thee drink? When saw we thee a stranger, and took thee in? or naked, and clothed thee? Or when saw we thee sick, or in prison, and came unto thee? And the king shall answer and say unto them, Verily I say unto you, Inasmuch as ye have done it unto one of the least of these my brethren, ye have done it unto me" Matt. 25:31-40.

Everything that is going on in your life you are attracting into your life. Your thoughts expand into the world around you. If you are thinking negative thoughts, negativity expands around you. Obversely when you think positive thoughts, positive things expand around you.

Learning to change the way you think will help you to change the things in your life. You can change your life, you can change the things in your life, you can do this by reprograming your life.

Basically whether you want it or not whatever you focus on in your mind and emotions (feelings) is what you are expanding into your life. Change the things you focus on and the things you focus on will change.

We attract into our lives those things who we are. As we live our lives and make the daily, even momentary decisions which shape our life's journey, we must remind ourselves the importance and power of our thoughts, feelings and behaviors. In order to attract into our lives the things which we want, we must first have our thoughts in alignment and plant the seeds thereby reaping the rewards of the harvest. By changing our thoughts we are able to reprogram our life and bring about the incredible things of our desires.

RESPONSIBILITY

When working on improving your life the very first thing you need to do is to take responsibility for it. Here is the part that is difficult for most people, YOU ARE RESPONSIBLE FOR YOUR LIFE, regardless of what other people may or may not have done, You have ultimately made the choices in your life which lead to where you are right now. It is correct you have no control over other people or their actions, but you have total complete control over yourself and your actions. No matter how hard you may try, you cannot change others, but you can change yourself. Everything you have done, every choice you have made, every action you make, every thought you have had is your responsibility. You are accountable for those things, no one else. Just as everyone else is accountable and responsible for their thoughts, choices and actions. Once you take ownership and responsibility for yourself, you begin to effect change for yourself.

Never underestimate your power to change yourself, and never overestimate your power to change others

~ Dr. Wayne Dyer ~

Accept the fact that you cannot control others and start making adjustments in your life which will lead toward improving your life. This is how you begin to reprogram your life.

Taking responsibility is hard. It is easy to say the reason you do something is because of other people's actions. "They won't leave me alone, they keep telling me to do the dishes and make my bed, If they would just leave me alone…." Does something like that sound familiar? Your actions and behaviors are your own, no one else's. You made the choices which got you to where you are in life. Yes, it is very possible you made the decisions based on the actions or choices of others. Regardless of the reasons or excuses, **you made the choice**. The fact remains, you made the decision. Because you made the decision, you have to own that choice and take responsibility for that decision.

There may be many things about life, that are
beyond your control.
But in the end, you have the power to choose
both your destination and
Many of your experiences along the way.
It is not so much your abilities, but your choices
that make the difference in life
~ Dieter F. Uchtdorf ~

You might be saying right now, "but it really wasn't my fault that _____ happened to me". It is very true, bad things do happen to good people, and the good people are not to blame for those bad things happening. I truly believe that there is evil in the world, after all Satan, our brother, is the God of this world. He blinds people's eyes and hides the gospel for those who are spiritually lost. 2 Corinthians 4:3-4

In all things there is opposition, if there is good, then there must be evil. Therefore if there are good men (people), then there must be evil men (people). Combine this with the gift of agency, which is afforded to all men (people) equally and the trouble really begins. So if the good people are allowed to make choices in their lives, then it must needs be that the evil people are allowed to make choices as well. That is the liberty afforded all of us by God and protected by our soldiers.

This is where the web of life becomes a bit sticky. When an evil person makes a choice, and yes it is a choice, to do something bad to another. Then the person who had the bad thing happen to them is forced to make choices based on the results of the evil doer. Where does that leave the good person? Many times this leaves the good person having to pick up the pieces and struggle. Even though the good person did not choose to have the evil done onto them, they now have choices to make. Based upon the choices made at this time and in the future determines the story of the person's life.

Many have asked, why does God not intercede and help the good person. This is one of those times when we don't know that answer, or maybe He did and we just don't know. Remember God works in mysterious ways. He sends His angels to help us on our journey. Those Angels may be the unseen kind of Heavenly helper or may be the visible kind such as your friend, a stranger, a therapist, or religious leader. Have faith and know that with God all things are possible. Do the best you can and trust He will make up the difference.

We face choices just about every minute of the day. Some of those choices are huge, like weather to marry or not. Most of them however are very small and we make them without thinking too much. Choices like walking down the sidewalk and stepping over a hole or going around it. Every single choice in our life has a consequence, some of those consequences are good and some are bad. Some choices have a clear good consequence and a clear bad consequence. Some have not so clear good or bad consequences, yet some only have bad consequences.

I believe it is best if we think through the consequences, even if it is only for a brief second, before we make the decision. Unfortunately many times we don't take the time to think it out and we make the choices quickly, instantly, irrationally or spitefully. This usually leads to negative consequences. When we analyze the choices to be made, we have to decide which consequence we are willing to live with, and make the decision. Either way we have to make a choice, because we have to choose no matter what may happen to us. Once we make the choice, we get to take the responsibility for the choice and the consequence which goes along with it.

Each of us is the product of all of our choices we have made in our lives. Our choices are based on the knowledge we have at the time the choice had to be made. We do the best with the information and knowledge we have at the time. Have you ever wondered why two different people make different choices when they are given the same situation. The answer to this question is the accumulation of knowledge and experience the person has at the time.

As we grow we acquire information from a multitude of sources. Sources such as: experience, school, friends, family, church, literally every interaction we have. Most of the time we are storing data that we don't even know we are putting into our memory banks. This information is used to make the choices throughout our life.

As we grow, all the experiences and teachings gained throughout our life build our character. It is our integrity and character which determine the choices we make in life. The most fundamental part of God's plan of happiness is the gift of agency. Agency is God's gift of choices, the ability to make choices. Even though God could actually control the path of our lives, because of the gift of agency, He must allow us to make choices independent of the consequences. He may guide, direct and influence us through the Holy Spirit or the use of Angels in our life. But He must ultimately allow us to make our own choices.

Every choice has a consequence, some may be good, others may be bad, yet a consequence still the same. Sometimes we may have to choose between two or more bad choices, with no good choice in sight. We make our choices based on the consequence we can live with . When we do not like the outcome of the choice, we cannot put the blame on someone else. The reality is we made the choice, the responsibility is ours, the accountability is ours, it is not the other persons responsibility or fault..

Every one of us goes through life carrying the consequences of our choices with us. We put them in a bag and carry them on our back everywhere we go. They become a weight, an anchor holding us to our past. This past weighs us down, it wears on us, often times we relive the past over and over not letting us move forward. I heard Dr. Dyer explain it like this. Our past is like large bags of manure, we carry around with us. Tossing the bag over our shoulder dragging it everywhere we go. Sometimes we pause, set the bag down, reach into it and smear it all over us, (this is like reliving the past over and over) then we wonder why our life stinks so much.

In order to move forward we need to give up our past. This is not as hard as it sounds. We make it seem harder than it really is. In order to give up our past we must first take responsibility for it. Even though it has been so easy, or convenient to blame others for the problems in our past. The truth remains we made each and every choice, therefore we are responsible for those choices and actions.

Once you have taken responsibility for your past, you have begun to make the shift in your life. Accepting the responsibility for your choices, allows you to accept the past for what it is. Understand the past is what it is, there is nothing you can do to change it. There is no point in reliving the past. It is time to accept it for what it is, take responsibility for your part in it. Learn from the events of the past so you can make better decisions in the future. Tie the bags up and leave it, you no longer need your past to hold you back. You can now move forward in life.

Begin now to make the shift in your life. Start the process of changing the way you think and you will begin to change your life. You have the power, you are in control of your life. You are now writing the next chapter of your amazing life.

ALIGNMENT

"I testify that when we embark upon or continue the incredible journey that leads to God, our lives will be better.

This does not mean that our lives will be free from sorrow. We all know of faithful followers of Christ who suffer tragedy and injustice—Jesus Christ Himself suffered more than anyone. Just as God makes the "sun to rise on the evil and on the good," He also allows adversity to test the just and the unjust. In fact, sometimes it seems that our lives are more difficult because *we are trying to live our faith.*

No, following the Savior will not remove all of your trials. However, it will remove the barriers between you and the help your Heavenly Father wants to give you. God will be with you. He will direct your steps. He will walk beside you and even carry you when your need is greatest.

You will experience the sublime fruit of the Spirit: "love, joy, peace, longsuffering, gentleness, goodness, [and] faith."

These spiritual fruits are not a product of temporal prosperity, success, or good fortune. They come from following the Savior, and they can be our faithful attendants even in the midst of the darkest storms."

Dieter F. Uchtdorf

When I speak of alignment, I speak of being aligned with God. Having our lives in align with the will of our Heavenly Father is what alignment really means.

Think of alignment similar to the way your car's tires are aligned with the rest of the vehicle. When everything is aligned the car travels down the road smoothly, the tires wear evenly, the car handles nicely, It corners better and overall it will last longer and your journey will be more enjoyable. When your vehicles tires are aligned properly you can even take your hands of the wheel for a brief minute and the car will travel straight. Just like in your life when you are aligned with God you can take your hands off the wheel for a brief minute and He will take control for a bit. When the alignment on your car is off, even by a little bit, the ride is much rougher. The tires wear poorly, it may mot corner properly. The steering wheel may vibrate and the overall journey is uncomfortable. You even get more exhausted from struggling with the steering wheel.

Our alignment with our Heavenly Father is much the same. When our lives are not aligned our journey is usually rougher and less enjoyable. We are often times much more exhausted because of all the stress and the extra work we are doing. When we follow God's plan our lives are happier. There is usually much less stress and the overall journey is more peaceful. Now don't get me wrong just because you have your life aligned with God's plan, you will not avoid all pain and suffering. However I will promise that when you are following God's plan and doing all you can, He will make up the difference and you will have peace in your heart. The Scriptures hold a promise, with God all things are possible.

What does it mean to be aligned with God? The simple answer is to live your life in accordance with the Plan of happiness laid out in the scriptures. Most of our lives we have heard the Sunday school answer to this question. Read the scriptures, go to church and say your prays. I know, right now you are saying how do these things help us get our lives in line with God's plan. Well let's think them trough for a minute.

We will start with going to church. The church house is a place where we can gather and learn more about God and His plan for us. We can fellowship with others who have similar beliefs. We can learn from each other, and believe it or not others are learning from you when you are there and participating in the activities. The simple act of showing up at church each week helps to strengthen habits in our life. Habits that not only happen at church but are in our daily life away from the church building. Keep in mind "going to church" is not just a Sunday and maybe Wednesday night thing. "Going to church" is a life style, it is what you do. A "church goer" can be the person who shows up on Sunday, then does not think of Jesus until next Sunday, when they show up at the church building to maintain their status as a "church goer". Or, you can live your life as a disciple of Christ. Going to church does not start and stop when you enter and exit the church house. Living your life according to the teachings of the gospel is what a "church goer" should do. So you see by aligning yourself with God, going to church is not a Sunday thing, it is a daily thing.

Another simple thing you can do to help align yourself with God is to read the Scriptures. The Scriptures contain the words of God, they literally tell us of the things we should and should not do in our lives. They contain the covenants we can make with our Heavenly Father. Along with the covenants He makes with us. Before you go and grab just any set of Scriptures I would suggest you do a bit of research. Remember it has been 2000 years since Jesus was here and taught the Gospel. Over that 2000 plus years the Scriptures have been translated many times. Kings and rulers have censored the texts and corrupted the meaning to match their personal and political agendas.

There are versions of the Scriptures which are closer to the original than others and thereby the message is less corrupted. They are a little more challenging to read as they are not written in modern English. The Scriptures written in modern language have lost some of the original meaning in the translation. The second part of this is, just reading the Scriptures is not enough. As you read you need to also study the text. Understand the meaning of the passage, pray about it. As you read, try to get a picture in your mind of what life was like at the time the scripture was written and the meaning of the words (which may not have the same meaning in today's language). You may re-read the same passage over and over so that you begin to understand the teaching contained within it. Make reading / studying the Scriptures a habit. Find a time you can designate every day to this effort. Your life will be blessed for doing this.

The other part of this triad is saying your prayers, it is so easy that we overlook it. So often we get caught up in our daily life that we forget to do the simple things. This reminds me of the lyrics of an 80's song: "I rush and rush until life's not fun". We all do this, we get so busy that we forget things. One of the most common things we forget or don't make the time for is prayer. The irony of this is incredible. You see, when you make the time to quiet your mind and spend time in prayer, you actually will be eliminating some of the natural chaos in your life and will find more time in your day.

In this world of advanced technology, we don't go anywhere without our cell phone. This phone in our pocket gives us a direct line to the world. But did you know you have always had a direct line to God. Prayer is just like the 'bat phone' to Heaven (had to throw in an 70's pop culture reference here). When it rings God answers, every time. Sometimes He will have a two way communication (if you are listening). Often times He is listening, but we are not, so He has to send his angels to help us. Never be afraid of getting on your knees, picking up that "bat phone" and have a conversation with your Father in Heaven. He will always answer, and it really is just that, a conversation. Prayer is the simplest form of speech. Simply start talking and let your thoughts flow.

I might suggest that we emulate the camel. The camel starts its day on its knees and ends its day on its knees. Starting our day in a thankful way sets the tone for the whole day. When you get out of bed, take a few moments to start your day on your knees. Thanking God in your prayers for all the blessings in your life. I promise you that you have many blessings. They may be hard for you to see right now, but you do have blessings. Just before you go to bed, end your night on your knees. Have an intimate conversation with your Father in Heaven. Being thankful for all the blessings in your life. Focus on the good things you have and the good things you and would like to do.

I would caution you not to focus on the negative things right before you go to bed. You see your brain is an amazing machine, the thoughts you have right before you go to sleep are some of the thoughts which fill your head at night, and now you have 8 hours to marinate on these thoughts. With this in mind, it may be wise to focus on the good things so your brain has pleasant thoughts to work on during the night.

There is something that I have noticed over the years, and that is when our prayers are of a 'give me, give me' nature, the answers to our prayers tend to be more of a 'give me, give me' nature. The opposite of this seems to be true as well. When our prayers are more like President Kennedy's address (words changed) "know not what your 'God' can do for you, but rather what you can do for your 'God'." When our prayers are more along the lines of 'how can I serve', the answers to our prayers are more along the lines of 'How can I serve you'. When we are in the services of others we are in the service of our God. When we live our lives in this manner the blessings we receive are amazing.

When we align our self with God, it allows for His plan of happiness to be fulfilled. It allows for the powers of Heaven to work their "magic" and quiet the chaos in our lives. By doing so it allows for the peace to flow thereby allowing us more time to have positive thoughts.

WILLINGNESS

As you start this journey, begin by becoming aware and realizing that with God all things are possible You can handle this process because you are not alone. Anything is possible, even the word impossible tells you this. Look closely at the word impossible, did you see it? Look closer, I'mpossible, not yet? Look closer, I'm Possible.

Nothing is
Impossible
the word itself says
I'm possible
-Audrey Hepburn

Throughout our life there are many doors which open and close. Some by our choice, some by others choices, and some by God's choice. Whichever the case may be these doors represent are opportunities, challenges, and growth. As doors close behind us others open in front of us. We may be a bit scared of what lies on the other side, we may be excited about it, we may be confused about it, we may even be terrified of it, but we must go through the door to get to what is on the other side. God will not give us things we cannot handle. There is a good chance we will need to lean on Him for the journey, but on the other side of those doors is an amazing journey. Step through hand in hand, He and you will begin the next leg of this incredible thing called life.

Sometimes we go in and out of the same doors over and over again not really getting anywhere in life this reminds me of the classic Scooby-Doo scene where there is a hallway of doors and the gang is going in one door and out the other zigzagging back and forth going to the same door over and over again but never making it out of where they are at. Quite often in life we do the same thing we continually go to the same door expecting something to be different, but yet we don't do anything different in our lives

Many of us spend our life in the comfort zone. We may like the place we are in life, we feel everything is good, and we don't want to challenge the status quo. Maybe we are staying in a job or a certain position in the company because we are comfortable. We know what to expect each day. We tell our self we will move on to another position or begin the next phase in our career after we accomplish _____. This is a lie we tell ourselves to justify the fact that we have become complacent. We are floating down the river 'denial'. As we all know, life does not allow us to continue on this path for long. If we do not make the decision to move forward, often times the decision is made for us. Maybe the company closes your office and now you are forced to take the next step. Maybe the co-worker next to you gets the promotion you thought you were working towards, but they got it for whatever reason, and now you are faced with a different work environment.

The difference between the person who stays in that comfortable place and the person who accepts some challenge in life and ventures forward is willingness. Having willingness is just that, being willing to make a change, to take a step out of that comfort zone. Willingness does not mean, not having fear and being confident. Yes it would be wonderful if we had full confidence in ourselves, and in the next phase of the journey and not being afraid of what lies ahead. In reality we all have some self-doubt, some level of lack of confidence, some amount of fear. These things are OK, they are completely normal. In fact I would suggest that they are necessary. They help to keep us grounded and help us to safely move forward on our journey.

Having willingness means having a mind that is open to new opportunities and not being tethered to anything. Dr. Phil asks a very important question, he asks: "How is that working for you?" When you ask yourself this question, you get one of two answers. It is working fine, if this is the case then there is no reason to make a change. If you answer, it is not, then logic says that you have to make some change. Having willingness means you are willing to open your heart, open your mind and allow for the process of change to begin. You can take this first step without overwhelming fear knowing you are not alone.

Sometimes the door to change is open and inviting, we can see what's on the other side. Most of the time the door of change is closed and closed doors are scary, we don't know what hides behind them. It is OK to be a bit afraid, embrace that emotion, have faith in the knowledge you have gained so far in life, Trust in the Lord and make the step. Being willing to make the steps forward which are necessary to make the change possible is within your grasp. You have the power, the knowledge and the ability to reprogram your life. Let's continue this journey together.

IDENTIFY THE CHANGE

You picked up this book and read this far into it because you have some level of desire to change your life. That is an amazing step. In fact it is very hard to admit that your life is going in a direction you don't want it to be going, and that you are in a place of vulnerability. For most people admitting they need help with anything is extremely difficult. I applaud you for being at the point where you are not only able to acknowledge needing help, but you actually want to change something in an effort to improve your life.

Now I have to ask you a little tougher question. What is it you want to change? I must caution you, If you answer "I want to change my life", that is too big of a task to tackle at one time. If you break it down to smaller portions we can handle that. Too big of a change at one time will be rejected by yourself and you will fail. I want to set you up for success. Therefore, we are going to break down the 'change my life' into smaller bite size portions or tasks. Things we can change and by making those changes you will begin to see a huge difference in your life.

In the resource section of this book there is a form called 'The Miracle Question'. This is a great time to answer that question. You may either use the form in the book or get out a piece of paper and answer the miracle question.

THE MIRACLE QUESTION

"Imagine you go to sleep tonight and you wake tomorrow morning. During the night a miracle happened and when you wake up, your most positive dreams for your future have come true. Remember, a miracle has occurred, so you are waking up to your life as you would ideally like it to be. At this point, you may have only quite hazy visions of your ideal future, so to help you be specific about what the real world changes would be for you, think about your answers to the following questions:

A. How do you feel when you wake?

B. What is the first thing you will do?

C. Your best friend arrives. Immediately, they notice that things have improved. What is that they will have noticed?

D. What happens next in your day?

E. Give a blow-by-blow account of the whole day of your ideal life when everything is just as you would ideally want it to be.

F. Would that be a typical day?

G. What would you be doing on the same day a week later?"

Great job, now that you have completed that little mind exhausting exercise, let's break it down and decipher the change you want to make. While you have the paper our, let's make a list. Maybe you have said you would like to change your life. What is it about your life you want to change? Write down what you want to change. Did you write one big thing or did you write several small things you would like to change? If you wrote down several small steps that is great. If you wrote down a big item, let's take a minute and break the big item into smaller steps or tasks.

Once you have these smaller tasks or items written down, take a minute to prioritize them. Putting the most important on top. By taking charge of the smaller chunks of your life, you will have a better chance of reprogramming your life. There is a very good chance you will need to make several small changes in your life rather than one large change. That is OK, actually you will be more successful and the changes will endure.

For our purposes pick one of the items on your list. Focus on that item for now, once you have made that change you can focus on another if you choose.

Identifying the change is very important to the process, I'm sure you understand you cannot accomplish something if you do not know what it is you want to accomplish. So let's take a minute and look at this from another angle just in case this step of the process is not completely clear yet.

You have decided that your life is not going the way you want it to be going. You have decided that you want to make a shift in your life. It is time for your life to take a different direction, but there is some behavior you are doing which you want to change. Identify that behavior, break it down.

What is the thought driving the behavior, where do you think this thought comes from? It is OK if you do not know the answers to these questions. What is important is that you identify the thing you want to change in your life. Make this as clear as you possibly can. Now that you have identified this, you have something to work on. You have done a lot of work so far by identifying the thing you want to change. Write it down, so you do not forget it, put it on paper so you have something to work towards.

Remember, our thoughts create our reality. The more energy we put into a thought, the more we think the thought, the more power we give the thought. The more power a thought gets the more it impacts our reality. This is where the rubber meets the road. When we change our thoughts we change our world. The way we perceive things truly does affect the way our life goes.

Do you still have that paper around? If not grab another piece, take a few minutes and reflect on your life at this point. Write down what your life will look like once you have made the changes you want to make. Don't worry, I'll wait for you. Just pick up the book when you complete the exercise. Do not skip this step. The power of visualization is very strong. Once you visualize something, it becomes real, it is now much easier to obtain. You can see the change in your brain and your mind can now make it a reality.

REPROGRAMING PARIDIGM

I am so glad you are still with me, you have read a lot of information and have hung in there. Now let's talk about how to reprogram your life. There is a paradigm (a model) by which you can learn to reprogram your life to get the results you want. As we work on reprograming your life, you will learn to change your life by changing your thoughts.

The Reprogram your life paradigm is going to challenge you, there will be times when you will not feel comfortable, quite possibly you may experience a bit of emotional pain. I don't tell you this to scare you, but rather to be honest with you. I believe when we know what we are getting into, we can make better decisions. Even though you will go through some discomfort, in the change process, it will all be worth it. You will realize a better life, the changes you make will improve your life, but you have to be ready to make the change.

How to change your life,
by changing your thinking.

Are you ready to make a change in your life? If the answer to this question is YES, or even "I Might Be", then keep reading . If the answer is to the question "Are you ready to make a change in your life?" is NO, then insert a book mark and close this book and come back to it when you are ready to make a change in your life. I will be right here waiting for you.

BELIEVE IN YOURSELF.

There is a process to change, steps to take, a paradigm, by following these steps in order and through to the end you will have the tools to effect real change in your life. Like I said earlier it will not be easy. I am reminded of a picture on the wall of the Church I attended in California. It was a picture of Jesus and under it read the inscription "I never said it would be easy, only worth it." With this in mind let's begin, shall we?

This is a good time to take a minute stretch your legs, get a drink of water, we are about to do some heavy lifting. You may want to get some paper and a pen, I am going to be asking you some question and you may want to write down the answers or take some additional notes. If you happen to have the reprogram your life workbook, you can use it for this part as well. Alright, let's get down to it.

Before you begin to put the paradigm to work in your life: Take an honest appraisal of your life, Educate yourself, Think realistically, use your friends and family, capitalize on your setbacks.

change your thoughts and you change your world.

I am not going to sugar coat it, making a real change in your life is hard. You are going to have to really examine your life, look at the behaviors you are doing, and examine the motivating factors behind the behaviors. You will be challenging yourself to do things that will probably not be comfortable for you. Let's face it, if it was easy you would not be reading this book. You would have already made the changes, and you would not be seeking information to improve your life.

I'm so glad you are still reading. You have already made the first hard choice; the choice to begin to make a change. Now that you are on a roll, let's keep it going. Let's jump into learning about the paradigm for change. The paradigm is a program built to help you reprogram your life. This paradigm is designed by utilizing proven techniques. Techniques refined through evidence based practices. Albert Ellis proved, if you change your thinking, you can change your life.

Many times we have thoughts which are incorrect. These negative thoughts, take us down a path where our behaviors cause us problems. Changing these negative thoughts into more positive thoughts, is the key to reprograming your life.

Don't Always Believe Everything You Think.

How do I change? I can't just start thinking positively and make everything all better. This is a very valid point. Change is not simply thinking positively. Yes positive thoughts are integral in the process. Putting the law of attraction to work in your life is part of the process. Remember the law of attraction we discussed it in chapter 3. Use the law of attraction to your benefit, in fact use every tool available to you to assist you along this journey.

The reprogram your life paradigm consist of 7 parts, working together to teach you how to change your life by changing your thinking.

- Is it working for me?
- What benefit am I getting?
- Create Motivation – a reason to change
- Set clear and manageable goals.
- Enlist Heavens Help.
- Track your progress
- Reward your progress

OK, You are ready for this, you have the strength, the courage, and the ability to make your life go the way you want it to go. Let us begin the journey together to reprogram your life.

Is it working for me?

How is that working for you? Dr. Phil made the phrase famous. This is such a great question. Where you are at in your life right now is the result of the accumulations of all the choices and behaviors you have made throughout your life. This is a point I want to make very clear, you are a

> "You are the product of all the choices you have made in your life"
>
> ~ Dr. Wayne Dyer ~

result of your choices. Do not blame others, you made the choices. Yes some of those choices may have been simply picking the lessor of two evils. Maybe even the choices you had to make were the result of someone else's choices, but never the less, you made the choice.

One of the greatest gifts the Lord has given humanity is agency. Agency is our ability to make choices, and this is a gift given to all freely. Along with this agency, comes consequences. Every choice has a consequence. Some of these consequences are negative, others are positive, still some may be neutral, neither positive nor negative. With these consequences to our choices comes the intertwining fabric of humanity. Some have called it the butterfly effect, that is when a person makes a choice, that choice has an effect on other people. Excuses or blaming spawn from this butterfly effect. One person makes a choice, the result of that choice puts another person in a position to make a choice. This choice creates a situation where we find ourselves being forced to make a choice. When we make a choice based on the actions of others and the result of our choice is negative, we tend to make and excuse. We blame others because it was their actions which caused the mess. Although true, we had to make a choice based upon the choices other have made, the responsibility for your choices remains with you.

Let's take a trip down the rabbit hole for a minute. We will take a detour into philosophy land and consider this: Every choice, every person makes is based on the choices of others. This goes back to the beginning of time. This is all part of the great plan of happiness. It is actually something we all agreed to before we came to earth. It is part of the test to see if we can make the choices which will lead us back to our Father in Heaven. It is not about whether the choice is right or wrong. It is about is the choice in alignment with the teachings of the Gospel. Sometimes the best choice happens to be the one with the worst consequences.

Alright go through the door, come out of the rabbit hole.

Back to the question at hand. The question "is it working for me?" , is one you need to ask yourself about the thinking which has brought you to this place. So pause for a moment and ask yourself , **Is it working for me?** Are the thoughts I'm having, taking me where I want to go?

YES – Turn to page   ~ 76 ~

NO – Turn to page ~ 133 ~

Hmmm, you answered YES to the question. Your thoughts are working for you? So, your thoughts are getting you to where you want to be? Ok, I feel very humble, you are reading this book just to listen to me. Thank you. I don't know what to say, except, I don't think you are being honest with yourself. So I'm going to ask you a follow up question. Are you 100% sure your thoughts are working for you? There exists NO possibility that your thoughts are not working for you? If there is ANY possibility your thoughts are not working for you, then the answer must be no. I'm going to suggest that by the simple fact you choose to read this book, they are not really working for you. That is OK, that is why we are here, to help you change your thinking to improve your life.

So now that you have thought about this question a little deeper, what is your answer? Has it been working for you? Are you 100% positive, your thoughts are taking you where you want to go? There exists NO possibility that your thoughts are not working for you?

YES - Turn to Page ~ 77~

NO - Turn to page ~ 79 ~
        (what benefit am I getting)

Ok so you have thought it through some more. You have decided that your thoughts are working for you. They are taking you to where you want to go. That is great. I can do no more. Close this book, place it on the table. I thank you for spending time with me. Go forth and do great things.

May God bless you.

Doug

What benefit am I getting?

Oh darn it, another question of self-introspection. I'm going to let you in on a little secret about human behavior. Every choice or behavior we make has a payoff. We get something out of it. So here is the time for you to ask yourself, what am I getting out this choice or behavior I want to change. Or maybe, you might ask yourself, why am I doing this? This may not be a simple question to answer.

Every behavior we do, we do it because we get something out of it. There is always a payoff of some sort, for our actions. Sometimes the payoff or reward for our actions is big, other times the benefit may be very small, no matter what the size of the payoff, there is still a reward of some kind. Many times the payoff is something we have become comfortable with. We get so accustom to it that the behavior becomes second nature, or automatic.

Our thoughts become our actions. Therefore the automatic behaviors are driven by automatic thoughts. Some of these automatic thoughts are beneficial, such as getting up, and brushing our teeth. Other can be harmful to us. Negative automatic thoughts like pitchin' a fit (that's a Texas thing, y'all might say throwing a tantrum), when you do not get your way, can cause negative consequences we don't like. Even though we don't like the consequence we continue to pitch a fit when we do not get what we want. We continue this behavior because it has become a habit. Habitual behaviors can be changed by utilizing the Reprogram your life paradigm.

We call these "Psychological Payoffs", They hook people into behavior patterns that provide some sort of psychological reward. Common examples of these types of behavior patterns include: overeating, procrastinating, problematic ways of interacting with other people, excessive spending and excessive TV or internet. People do not typically tend to keep these patterns unless they are getting something good from the behavior. Understanding what psychological need you are fulfilling with the unwanted behavior will help you to begin to move forward with changing the behavior.

Let's look at some common payoffs for people. Payoffs typically come in two varieties:

1: Getting more of something you want.
2: Experiencing less of something you don't want. (avoiding difficult thoughts, numbing negative emotions, or escaping from difficult situations or tasks.)

There are different types of payoffs. There are emotional payoffs, thought payoffs, physical payoffs and situational payoffs. Let's just take a minute and explore each so you can get a feel for them.

Emotional payoffs

For emotional payoffs ask yourself a few questions.

- Does the behavior you want to do less of provide any positive emotions? If so, which ones?
  - Calmness, soothing, relaxation, joy, excitement, interest.
- Does doing the behavior reduce your negative emotions? If so, which ones?
  - Anxiety, fear, tension, shame, anger, loneliness, sadness, guilt?

Sometimes the emotional payoffs will be very mild, such as provide a mild sense of interest or excitement, or maybe decreasing your anger a little bit.

One of the most common payoffs often associated with unwanted behavior is reduced anxiety or tension. There are a lot of different types of unwanted behavior help people temporarily reduce feelings of anxiety.

Thought payoffs

Thought payoffs come in so many different types we cannot go through them all here, so we are just going to talk about a few to get your mind going.

- Distracting yourself

    o This is when you distract yourself from thinking about something that is difficult to think about. For example, numbing yourself with media can be an effective distraction from thinking about aspects of your life and relationships.

- Being the master of your own destiny

    o "I'm an adult and I can do what I want". This often applies to unwanted behaviors that involve breaking your own or other people's rules (spending money that's not in your budget or breaking a diet). There's nothing wrong with the deep psychological need of wanting to do what you want, but if this need is popping up in your life in unwanted ways it might not be getting fulfilled in more healthy ways in other areas of your life.

- How you see yourself as a person and how others see you.

  o Let's say it's really important to you that other people know you're a nice, fair, generous, or fun person. If that's important to you it will be a powerful motivator of your behavior. For example, if you view spending money freely as part of your fun-loving/carefree persona this might lead to you spending more money than you can afford. Or, wanting to be perceived as nice might lead you to be too generous in helping others. If doing an unwanted behavior, validates your sense that you're nice, fair, generous, fun (or whatever it is that's important to you) then it is most likely an important psychological payoff.

- Deserving thoughts

  o Deserving thoughts are when doing the unwanted behavior validates that you "deserve" the good outcomes that come with the unwanted behavior. Maybe you deserve to have the thrill of buying nice things, you deserve to treat yourself, you deserve to relax. Deserving payoffs are often very powerful motivators of behavior if underneath you perceive yourself as having low worth (low self-esteem).

Physical payoffs

Some types of unwanted behavior have physical payoffs. For example for the short period after you eat a high sugar snack it might have a big payoff of increasing energy and reducing tiredness. This intense short term physical payoff is likely to be very powerful in keeping you doing that unwanted behavior during times when you're tired.

Situational payoffs

- What happens after you do the unwanted behavior?
  - Yelling at your child or partner might be effective in getting them to do what you

need in the short term (even it's not helpful for those relationships in the long term).

- If you yell at your partner does he or she stop nagging you?

- Does doing the unwanted behavior (at least temporarily) "get you out of" something you don't want to do or something that would be difficult to do?

- Does sabotaging your relationships mean you avoid relationship closeness and commitment issues that would be difficult for you?

These are some of the most common payoffs we get for our behaviors, hopefully they help you to figure out what you are getting out of the behavior.

Earlier you identified the thing you wish to change. You asked yourself was it working for you. Your answer to that question was, it is not working for me. Now you are examining the driving force behind it. You are figuring out what you are getting out of this thought. Now that you have identified the payoff you get from the thought, it is time to move on to the next step.

Do you still have that piece of paper? If not grab another. It is time to make a declaration. Write down on the paper.

"I did (this) _____
_____ and it did not work, now I'm going to do _____ .

Create motivation

The reason we continue to do the things we do is because we are comfortable. So now you may be asking, What do you mean I am comfortable? No, I am not comfortable, I'm miserable, so why do I keep doing it. The simple answer is; *The comfortable misery we know is better than what we do not know*. Making changes in our life is difficult, we have to have a rational reason to change. A little while back, I had a friend told me " in order for people to change they need to have some sort of pain." Pain is an incredible motivator. The pain does not always have to be physical, many times it is emotional pain. My friend continued with, "the reason people don't change is because they are getting away with it." If we are not seeing any problems with our actions/thoughts, then we don't think anything is wrong with it.

> You can't give away what you don't have
>
> ~ Dr. Wayne Dyer ~

In order to effectively make a change in your life, you must have a rational reason to change, some kind of motivation to push you through the change process. Sometimes this motivation or reason to change is built in by life, maybe a significant person in your life tells you "If you keep doing this, I'm leaving and I'm not going to be around for you." Other times there is no built in reason and you will need to create one.

Start by asking yourself, why do I want to make this change?

Remember a little while ago when you did that visualization exercise, where you wrote down what your life would look like once you made the changes you want. Maybe that exercise can help you create the motivation you need. Motivation comes in many different forms. It looks different for everyone. Find that motivation, give yourself a reason to make the changes. Be careful not to make the reason generic like 'to have a better life'. Something like that is way too generalized. Your motivation needs to be very specific and tailored to your wants and desires. Remember we get a payoff, we get something for every behavior. So create a payoff that is big enough for you to follow through and actually do something different. Create a situation where the 'pain' of not changing is greater that the 'pain' of making the change.

This is a good enough time as any to talk about vision boards. Have you ever heard of a vision board? They can be pretty powerful tools in our lives to help us stay on track, to generate a constant reminder of what we want , and to generate motivation in our life. They give us direction in our life, similar to a road map. They give us a look at where we want to go. Creating a vision board is very simple. You can make your vision board as simple or as complex as you like.

A vision board is a place for you to put images of what you want to achieve in life. Sort of like snapshots of your future goals achieved. Psychology has proven that images are very powerful. I am sure you have heard the saying 'a picture is worth a thousand words', it is true. You can look at a picture and invoke memories and thoughts. You can see the final destination and many times the path along the way.

You can use a note board and pin images to it, or you can simply tape them to the mirror. If you

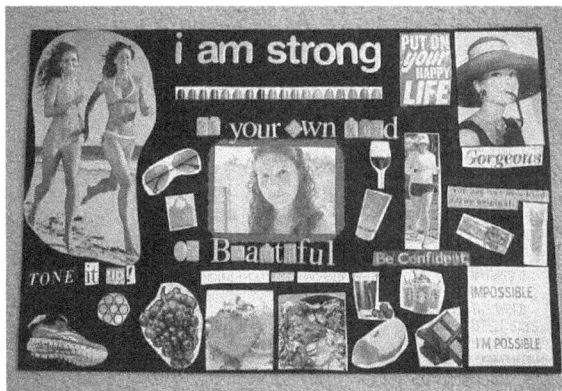

are one of those very crafty people, you can create a custom scrap book style page. Whatever your choice is, make it yours. On the vision board place images which will remind you of the goals you have set. Images that will generate the motivation to keep going when the struggle begins. Images that will give you the push to make it over that hump. Once you create the vision board, place it in a place you can see it every day. The daily reminder will give you bursts of motivation to keep going.

While we are on this topic, let's take a minute to talk about affirmations. Affirmations are also very powerful tools, and they can also find their way onto you vision board. Affirmations can be both positive and negative. It is probably a no brainer, we are going to talk about positive affirmations. There is a list of some in the resource section in this book to help spur your ideas.

I AM IN CHARGE OF HOW I FEEL AND TODAY I AM CHOOSING HAPPINESS.

Don't overthink this, a positive affirmation is just a positive thought or message to yourself. Something like "I have the ability and strength to make real changes in my life". When you read your affirmation over and over every day your mind begins to believe it and it becomes real. Hey look at that, you just learned how to play a mind trick on yourself. Psychology can be so cool. Create a positive affirmation for yourself and pin it to your vision board.

Ok you have used a lot of brain power, now is a good place to take a break. If you have not already done so, take a pause right now and create your motivation. If you want to use the vision board start your vision board with a picture to help with your motivation and a positive affirmation. Once you have recovered from the mental work out, pick up this book again and let's work on setting clear and attainable goals.

Great job so far.

Set clear and attainable goals

You cannot solve a problem with the same mind that created it

~ Ralph Waldo Emmerson ~

Setting a goal is a very powerful tool to help us make changes. By setting a goal, it gives us something to set our sights on, and achieve. The trick to making goal setting work is to set goals which we can actually achieve. If you set the goal too high and cannot actually do it, then you have set yourself up for failure, and you are just going to create more anxiety and stress.

So now you're ready to set a goal, but what would be a good goal to set? What goal can you set that will help you make the change you want? That is a great question, I'm glad you asked. You could just pick a goal out of the air that sounds like it will help you get there, or you could do a bit of planning and find a goal that will actually help you make the change.

When you set a goal, make sure it is something you can actually do, **it is achievable**. You may need to challenge yourself a bit, but not so much that you will get frustrated and quit. If you were to set a goal to run

5 miles, you may not be able to run 5 miles right this minute, in order to be able to actually run 5 miles you need to work up to it. You might start slow, by walking for a ½ mile, then 1 mile. Once you reach that goal you might start jogging for a half mile, then 1 mile, then 2 miles, then 3 miles, then 4 miles, and finally 5 miles. By setting smaller obtainable goals you were able to get to your big goal of running 5 miles. If you started off with a goal to run the whole 5 miles, you most likely would have been like the majority of people and quit because it was too difficult.

Now you may be asking ok, I know what I want to change, but how do I choose goals to help me get there? The most effective way to set goals is to start from the end and work backwards. Steven Covey said "start with the end in mind" imagine yourself as though you have already made the change. Now work backwards, what do you need to achieve to get there?

Let's look at an example. If you want to become more educated and graduate with a bachelor's degree and you currently have a high school diploma, start with the end in mind.

- In order to graduate from the university, I actually have to get to the university,

- so I must apply to the university.
- Before I can apply for the university, I need to graduate from college.
- In order to graduate from college, I need to get into college.
- In order to get into college, I need to apply.
- In order to apply, I need to take the SAT.
- Before I can take the SAT I need to schedule a date to take the SAT.
- I need to study for the SAT.
- I need to get a study guide for the SAT, before I begin studying.

(I simplified this list for the sake of time, there are several other steps I omitted. Be sure to put all the steps into your plan)

Now that you have worked from the end backwards, you have discovered a series of goals. This series of goals builds upon themselves from easier to more difficult. Take the list you created and flip it, make the last first and the first last, to create your series of goals. Here is what this series of goals might look like:

- Get a study guide
- Study for the SAT
- Schedule the SAT
- Apply to college
- Graduate from college
- Apply to the university
- Graduate from the university

By starting with the end in mind and working backwards, you can discover the goals which will help you be successful in making the change you want to make.

This is a great time for you to set your goal or series of goals. Imagine yourself as if you have already made the change you want to make. Take a look back at the miracle question to stimulate you imagination. Now set this book down, get a piece of paper and a pen, starting with the image of yourself where you want to be and work backwards, writing down the things you need to achieve to make that change. Keep working backwards until you get to the point at which you are at right this moment. Now invert the list making the first one last and the last one first. (just like in the Bible, the first shall be last and the last shall be first) Congratulations, you have just created a series of achievable goals to help you make that change you want to make.

Write the goals down starting with the first thing you need to do. Put them in order from first to last. If possible add dates by when you would like to accomplish each one. Keep in mind the plan will be fluid, ever changing, the dates can change, that is ok as long as there is forward movement.

Many people feel that life is just happening to them and they have no control over where life takes them. The biggest reason they feel this way is that they do not have any goals. They do not have something to shoot for. They have not spent much time thinking about what they want from life. If you want to take control of your life and make it go where you want to go, you have to have a plan for your life.

How to Set a Goal

*First, consider what you want to achieve, and then commit to it. Set **SMART** (specific, measureable, attainable, relevant and time-bound) goals that motivate you and write them down to make them feel tangible. Then plan the steps you must take to make your goal happen, and cross off each one as you work through them.*

You would not set out on a journey across the country without having a plan and a map to help you get there. This map keeps you on track and guides your journey in the direction you want to travel. A good life plan is a map for your life, just like for that journey across the country, A life plan will guide you and keep you on track to help you get where you want to go on this journey we call life.

A very powerful process to motivate yourself to turn your ideas of your future into reality is **goal setting**.

The whole process of setting goals puts you in control of your life and allows you to choose where you want to go. When you know exactly what you want to achieve, you know what you need to concentrate on. You will also be able to spot distractions that can lead you astray.

The Process of Goal Setting

There are multiple steps to set your goals:

• The first thing you need to do is develop the "big picture". This is what you want your life to look like. As you develop this big picture, you will identify large scale goals that you want to achieve.

• Next, you break these large-scale goals down into smaller goals, much like steps to get you to your larger goals.

• Once you have developed the big picture, identified the large-scale goals and the steps to get you there, it is time to put the plan into action.

By starting with the end in mind and working backwards, you can build a plan of goals to get you to where you want to be.

The big picture may be 10 years or so down the line. As you work backwards, your goals may be 5 years goals, next year goals, next month goals, and next week goals, all the way to today goals. You put

Why Set Goals?

Top-level athletes, successful business-people and achievers in all fields all set goals. Setting goals gives you long-term vision and short-term motivation. It focuses your acquisition of knowledge, and helps you to organize your time and your resources so that you can make the very most of your life.

By setting sharp, clearly defined goals, you can measure and take pride in the achievement of those goals, and you will see forward progress in what might previously have seemed a long pointless grind. You will also raise your self-confidence, as you recognize your own ability and competence in achieving the goals that you have set.

them all down on paper and start working towards them.

To create a balanced life, try to set goals in all areas of your life. Look at the following categories for inspirations, add your own categories that fit your life and are important to you.

Career – What level do you want to reach in your career, or what do you want to achieve?

Financial – How much do you want to earn, by what stage? How is this related to your career goals?

Education – Is there any knowledge you want to acquire in particular? What information and skills will you need to have in order to achieve other goals?

Family – Do you want to be a parent? If so, how are you going to be a good parent? How do you want to be seen by a partner or by members of your extended family?

Artistic – Do you want to achieve any artistic goals?

Attitude – Is any part of your mindset holding you back? Is there any part of the way that you behave that upsets you? (If so, set a goal to improve your behavior or find a solution to the problem.)

Physical – Are there any athletic goals that you want to achieve, or do you want good health deep into old age? What steps are you going to take to achieve this?

Pleasure – How do you want to enjoy yourself? (You should ensure that some of your life is for you!)

Public Service – Do you want to make the world a better place? If so, how?

Faith – Are you satisfied with your activity level in the Church? Do you want to start attending Church?

A great way to start is to brainstorm the categories. Write down as many ideas that come to your mind. Once you have several in each category, go back and narrow them down to the ones you really want to use to guide your life. Trim down your goals until you have a few to focus on. You cannot tackle too much at one time, smaller chunks are more manageable and more realistic to achieve.

As you reduce your list, make sure you keep the goals you really want to work on, not ones other people want you to work on. You are more likely to achieve your goals if they are YOUR GOALS.

Now that you have developed your lifetime goals, break down the smaller goals you will need to reach and accomplish in order to reach your lifetime goals. Break these down for each of your lifetime goals into a five year plan, then a 1 year plan, then a 6 month plan, continue working backwards creating the steps you need to complete in the next month, week, all the way to tomorrows goals.

Remember, your goals and actions steps are not carved in stone. The plan will be fluid, as you reach a goal and head to the next, things in life may change and you may need to re-adjust some of your goals. That is OK; remember it is a map to get you to your goals.

Once you have set your goals, create a *Daily Task List* of things that you should do today to work towards your lifetime goals.

At an early stage, your smaller goals might be to read books and gather information on the achievement of your higher-level goals. This will help you to improve the quality and realism of your goal setting.

Finally review your plans, and make sure that they fit the way in which you want to live your life.

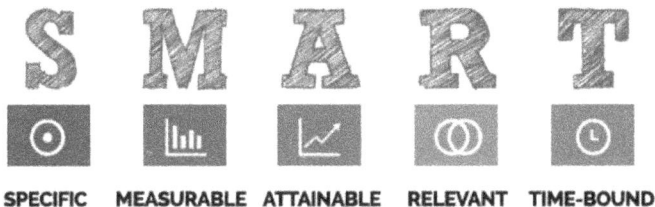

SPECIFIC   MEASURABLE   ATTAINABLE   RELEVANT   TIME-BOUND

SMART Goals

A useful way of making goals more powerful is to use the SMART mnemonic. While there are plenty of variants (some of which we have included in parenthesis), **SMART** usually stands for:

S – Specific (or Significant).

M – Measurable (or Meaningful).

A – Attainable (or Action-Oriented).

R – Relevant (or Rewarding).

T – Time-bound (or Trackable).

Staying on Course

Once you have decided on your first set of goals, keep the process going by reviewing and updating your Daily Task List on a daily basis.

Periodically review the longer-term plans, and modify them to reflect your changing priorities and experience.

(A good way of doing this is to schedule regular,

For example, instead of having "to sail around the world" as a goal, it is more powerful to use the SMART goal "To have completed my trip around the world by December 31, 2020." Obviously, this will only be attainable if a lot of preparation has been completed beforehand!

Tips for setting goals

~The following tips will help you set effective, achievable goals ~

• **Use positive statements** - State each goal in a positive manner. Rather than "Don't make this stupid mistake," state it by saying "Execute this technique well."

• **Be precise** - You need to be able to measure your achievements, so be precise, using dates, times and amounts. This way you know exactly what you need to achieve and can take satisfaction when you achieve it.

• **Set Priorities** - When you have several goals you can easily get overwhelmed. By setting priorities, you can organize the tasks according to importance.

• **Write down goals** - When you write it down, you can take ownership and are putting it into your memory.

• **Keep goals small** - If a goal is too large, it will seem overwhelming and you will put it off and never accomplish it. When you use smaller goals, you will feel the progress as you check off the steps on the road to your lifetime goals.

• **Set performance goals** - Set goals that you have as much control over as possible. If the outcome is out of your control, it will be very hard on you.

• **Set realistic goals** - Make sure the goals you set are realistic. They must be achievable. If you set a goal that you cannot reach, you will become discouraged and stop. Sometimes, we under-estimate what is required to achieve a goal. Do not worry when a goal is too hard or unrealistic, you can modify it; break it down into smaller achievable goals.

• **Achieving your goals** - As you progress through your journey, take note of the achievements you have made. Reward yourself accordingly when you have checked off your goals.

After achieving a goal, review the remainder of your goals on your plan.

• **Did you achieve your goal to easily?** Consider making your next goal a bit harder.

• **Did the goal take a long time to achieve, or was it too difficult?** Consider making the next a bit easier to achieve.

• **Did you learn something that makes you want to change your goals?** Do so.

• **Did you notice you have a skill deficit?** Even though you achieved your goal. Decide if you need to set a goal to learn new skills.

As you learn things along the journey, feed that back into the process of setting your future goals. Remember the goal process is fluid and changes as you go and as your needs change. As you grow in knowledge and experience, your goals may change or some may no longer be needed. It is okay to delete goals no longer needed. Adjust your goal plan regularly to keep you on the right track.

How do we enlist Heaven's help

Placing a call to the Heaven Hotline allows for the power of Heaven to lighten the load. There is absolutely nothing wrong with asking for help, and no better place to ask for that help, than from Heaven above. This sounds like a daunting task, which in all actuality is not that difficult at all, unfamiliar maybe, but not difficult.

Prayer is the direct connection to Heaven, if you are not familiar with praying, just like any new thing, it can be a bit scary. So let's take a minute and walk through prayer together.

Find yourself a quiet place where you can be alone. Kneel down on your knees. Take a deep breath and relax. Now simply have a natural conversation with your Father in Heaven. Address Him, Dear Heavenly Father. Thank Him for all that you have, for the good things and everything you are thankful for. Next just talk with Him as if you are conversing with a person you respect. Have a natural conversation, asking Him to help you, with your struggles and for guidance. When you are finished, simply close in the Name of Jesus Christ, Amen.

The powers of "Heaven can literally move mountains, never underestimate the help you can receive from God, If you ask with honest and real intent, you will receive the help you need. "Ask, and it shall be given you; seek, and ye shall find; knock, and it shall be opened unto you. For every one that asketh receiveth; and he that seeketh findeth; and to him that knocketh it shall be opened. (Mathew 7:7-8) Priesthood power is the strongest force on Earth, through prayer and the power of the priesthood miracles can be performed.

We talked about the positive powers of Heaven and we know there is opposite in all things. Does that mean there is opposing spiritual forces? Yes, absolutely, undoubtedly, YES. Before the world began we all were part of a grand council in Heaven, where we chose to follow a plan presented by Jesus. A plan where all mankind comes to earth, is tested, proves themselves and returns to live in Heaven forever.

There was a choice presented, and we all had the opportunity to choose, some of our brothers and sisters, unfortunately chose to follow Lucifer. His charismatic personality and leadership was very enticing to some and they joined him in his plight. These souls never received a body to come to earth and became the dark angels. They are the ones who assist Lucifer in his attempts to drag us into his

> The ancestor to every action is a thought
>
> ~ Ralph W. Emmerson ~

world. We can all use the powers of heaven to battle the forces of evil in our lives.

Begin with prayer

By simply asking you can enlist the powers of Heaven. I know that almost sounds too easy. But in fact it really is that simple. Our Heavenly Father wants to help us, all we have to do is ask. Ok so there is a bit of a trick to receiving the help, but it is not hard. "…and if ye shall ask with a sincere heart, with real intent, having faith in Christ, he will manifest the truth of it unto you, by the power of the Holy Ghost." (Moroni 10:4) What does that really mean, a contrite spirit? Contrite (spirit) heart means "to be completely penitent, feeling remorse and affected by guilt, deeply regretful and wishing to atone for sin." A sincere heart means you really want it. You want it because your thoughts and desires are in line with the thoughts of Heavenly Father. If your thoughts / prayers are contrary to the will of our Father in Heaven you will not receive it. Heavenly Father can give us all that he has, as long as we are in line with the plan of happiness.

"Prayer is a supernatural gift of our Father in Heaven to every soul. Think of it the absolute supreme being, the most all-knowing, all-seeing, all-powerful personage, encourages you and me, as insignificant as we are, to converse with Him as our Father..... It matters not our circumstances, but we humble or arrogant, poor or rich, free or enslaved, learned or ignorant, loved or forsaken, we can address Him. We need no appointment. Our supplication can be brief or can occupy all the time needed, it can be an extended expression of love and gratitude or an urgent plea for help. He has crested numberless cosmos and populated them with worlds, yet you and I can talk with Him personally, and He will ever answer. " – Richard G. Scott.

*"In this life we have to make many
choices – some are very important
choices, some are not. Many of our
choices are between good and evil. The
choices we make, however determine to a
large extent our happiness or our
unhappiness, because we have to live
with the consequences of our choices.
Making perfect choices all the time is not
possible. It just doesn't happen. But it is
possible to make good choices we can
live with and grow from. When God's
children live worthy of divine guidance
they can become free forever, knowing
good from evil; to act for themselves and
not be acted upon."* - James Foust.

God will help you along this journey. Jesus Christ
will walk beside you and lift you when you need
support. All you need to do is ask, enlist Heavens help
on your journey and your burdens will be lightened.

Track your progress

As you venture down the journey of making changes in your life it is easy to lose track of where you are going and where you have come from. By setting goals and having them written down you can check them off as you achieve them. This will help you to keep track of where you are going. Along the journey though be sure to track your progress.

Track the things you have completed, marking your successes along the way. It is very empowering to be able to see what you have accomplished. Sometimes we can feel a bit overwhelmed with the daunting tasks we are tackling and we lose sight of the great things we have already accomplished. Take a few minutes to review occasionally the progress you have made so far. This will feed your EGO a bit and give you more gas to keep moving forward.

Tracking your progress can be done simply by having a to do list, I prefer a daily prioritized task list. There one in the resource section of this book you can use if you like. There is also a great planner available for free

✓	ABC	Prioritized Daily Task

download from resources.psychfit.net. If you write your goals or series of goals down and as you accomplish them do not erase them but rather just check them off. This allows you the option to go back and review the things you have accomplished. By doing so you are able to empower yourself with pride of accomplishment. We tend to forget the things we have done and this gives you the opportunity to review those great accomplishments.

Reward your progress

By nature we humans tend to resist change, unless there is some kind of reward for it. Remember when we talked about payoffs, that is a great way to reinforce the change process. Earlier you identified the payoff you were receiving for the behavior you no longer want to do. You used that information to create the motivation to make the change. At this point in the process we can use the same process to reinforce the change. It is now time to create a reward for changing. Before, you associated a negative consequence with the behavior you wanted to change, let's create a positive reward for doing the new behavior.

Many times the new behavior or thought pattern will have a built in reward system. Something along the lines of feeling better, having less stress, or maybe a better relationship with a loved one. Other times we have to create the reward. The simplest way to create a reward to reinforce the new behavior or thought is to actually give yourself something, It sounds very simple and sort of like bribing yourself and it is exactly that. Every time you do the new behavior or thought give yourself something. A word of caution at this point, do not make it food or something expensive or elaborate. Something small and preferably something that does not cost money is best. Here are some ideas of rewards you might use: an extra few minutes with your pet, a walk by the lake or in the park, a sticker on a board, a quarter in a jar, the list is endless, just make is something you enjoy.

Maybe the change you want to make is going to need to be done in steps, that is ok. In fact that is a good thing, smaller chunks are easier to work with and you will have better results. You will also see the effects of the change process a bit faster if you are doing it in small steps. When this is the case, be sure to reward yourself for the accomplishments along the way. You probably set a series of goals, as you check off the goals give yourself a reward. This way you can enjoy the hard work you have been doing.

When you take the little bit of time to reward yourself for the progress you have been making you are reinforcing the new behavior or thought over time you will be moving the new behavior or thought from your conscious mind into your habitual mind and it will become automatic. The amount of time it takes to make this a permanent change is different for all people. There is an old saying, I am sure you have heard it; "Practice makes perfect". The problem is, the saying is wrong. In reality "Practice make PERMANENT".

The more we do something does not necessarily make us better at it, however it does cement it into our habitual mind and thereby it becomes permanent. So practice the new behavior or thought over and over and you will make it permanent.

YOUR BACKPACK

I'm sure you have heard some motivational speaker talk about *"the tools in your toolbox"*. This metaphor has been used by so many over the years to describe the coping skills or strategies people use in life. I don't like *"the tools in your toolbox"* metaphor. These "tools" in your box are supposed to be things you carry with you. Toolboxes sit on the counter in the garage, no one carries a tool box around with them. If you do not carry your toolbox, you will not have the tools with you when you need them. Ok, so it is supposed to be an imaginary toolbox where you store the mental tools you have learned. But what if you could "actually" take your tools with you?

Just about everyone has carried a backpack at one time or another in their life. Personally I have my backpack with me just about all the time. My backpack is real, not just imaginary, and very handy. May I suggest you carry a backpack with you as well. In my backpack I have all my mental "tools", or coping skills, such as breathing techniques, taking a walk, grounding, meditation…. I also have plenty of room to store new coping skills I learn along my journey. Here is the best part of my backpack, I can put real stuff in it. Yes coping skills are real, but you don't necessarily need a place to store them, other than your mind. Unless of course if you write them down in a notebook an place it in your backpack. That is a great Idea.

In my backpack I have a small notebook, which has the coping skills I have learned written down. I can go to this notebook when I am stressed or anxious and remind myself of the coping skills I can use to improve my mood and reduce stress and anxiety. You see, when we get stressed or anxious our brain has trouble operating smoothly and many times we forget about the "cool tools" we have learned. By having my little notebook in my backpack I can remind myself of the ways to deal with the stress and anxiety.

Along with these great mental coping skills we have, there are so many other items that help us deal with life. Carrying a backpack is a great way to have these things ready and at hand when you need them. Everyone's backpack will contain different things. Fill your backpack with the things that help you. Here are a few items which may find their way into your backpack.

Note Book & Pen

A note book is a great place to write down you're the coping skills you learn along your journey. You can also use it to make important notes so you don't forget things as life gets busy.

Stress balls

Although they are great to throw at people who stress you out, that is not what they are designed for. Having one available to squeeze when you start feeling anxious or stressed will help reduce the negative feelings by giving your mind something else to focus on as well as your hand something to exercise. Thereby burning off some of those stress chemicals.

Aroma Therapy

Smells are so very powerful. There has been so many studies in using smells to overcome problems, reduce stress, calm, etc.. You can carry some essential oils with you to use when the time is right. I would just ask a small favor for me and many of society. Be cautious with the smells or odors you use. Smells do not affect every person the same way. You may find something soothing and another may find the same smell annoying or it may even cause them to have a headache. Use the smells wisely and keep to the adage "less is better".

Journal

Writing is a great coping skill. It gives you a place to voice your concerns, work out some stress, make notes on how you handle something, record events that triggered problems so you can learn to work with future issues that will arise. By keeping a journal and pen in your backpack you will be able to record thoughts and other information more closely to its occurrence. This way it will be more accurate and helpful for you in the future.

Playdough

Playdough is an awesome thing to keep with you. You can squish it, stretch it, mold it, and squish it again. You can form it into things that stress you and squish it symbolizing squishing your stress.

Water bottles

Very few people drink the proper amount of water each day. You should drink half of your body weight in ounces of water each day. So if you weigh 200 pounds, half of that in ounces is 100 ounces. Divided by 16 ounces (a standard water bottle), that equals 6 water bottles at a minimum. If you are active or it is hot, you will need to drink more water. Water is also a great tool when we are anxious. Simply taking a drink of cool water will help to lower the anxiety we are feeling.

Medications

Many people take medications on a regular basis or maybe have a prescription which is on a as needed basis. If you have medications, having some in your backpack for the times when you need them will be very helpful for you.

Book / Kindle

Reading is a great coping skill. Of course you cannot read if you do not have a book with you. Your backpack is a great place to keep a book at the ready for times when you can take it out and read a few pages.

Diet

Ok, you cannot keep your diet with you in your backpack. However there are so many times while we are out running around doing errands and such that we get so busy we forget to take the time to eat. Or maybe you are on a specialized nutrition plan and eating at a fast food restaurant is not really an option for you, You can carry some nutrition bars with you and they will hold you over until you can properly take care of your nutrition needs.

Meditation

Meditation changes our relationship with our thoughts and feelings. Often people overthink meditation, it is not as difficult as many people think. Here is a simple way to meditate which you can do anyplace any time and only takes a few seconds.

Simply take a few seconds and focus on your breath, notice it entering your lungs and leaving your lungs, do not try to change your breathing, simply notice it. Focus on your breathing for a few seconds. That is it, you just did a very simple mediation. You can expand upon this by adding some calming music which you may have on a MP3 player in your backpack.

Hopefully you can see how a backpack can be so much more useful than an imaginary "toolbox". I would encourage you to take a backpack with you and keep those things in it which will help you on your life journey.

CONCLUSION

Wow that was a lot of work, but you made it, I am proud of you, It takes a lot of courage to be able to work through the discovery process you just went through and to follow the journey to the end. I am sure there were many times along the path where you thought to yourself, This is tough I don't want to do this, but you stuck with it and now you are on the way to a better life.

Reprograming our thoughts truly does help us to change our lives. Study after study show that our thoughts control our actions. When we change the way we think we truly change our lives. Remember when we talked about practice making permanent? It is true, take the time to continually practice your new way of life so that you can make it permanent for yourself.

"If you believe you can or you believe you cannot, either way you are right"

~ Henry Ford ~

THE SECRET TO MY SUCCESS

"What is the secret to your success in life?"

People are always asking me, what is the secret to your success in life? To tell you the truth, I don't know what the secret is, but I can tell you what has worked for me. It took me a while to put my finger on it. Maybe, I am just not as bright as I think I am. Because, now that I truly understand it, it seems like a no brainer.

Secrets are usually meant to be guarded and kept to yourself, but I am going to let you in on my secret. Well do not let me lie to you, it really is not a secret. You see, the reason my life has gone the way it has to this point, and why I have enjoyed to the blessings in my life which I have, is all because of the relationship I have with a very good friend of mine.

I spent the early part of my life, up until I was 21 with my friend being far off, and not really inviting Him into my life much. Even though I did not ask Him to be around, or take part in my life, He was always there, watching me from the distance and making sure I did not stray too far way. Then through some common friends, I started hanging out with my friend a lot more, and inviting Him to join me and my friends, in our day to day activities. Ever since then, I have enjoyed a blessed life. Do not get me wrong, not a life free of troubles. But, the troubles I have, I know I can handle them, because I have good friends to stand by me.

You probably know my good friend, because He is in your life as well. His name is Jesus Christ. Hopefully you are a bit brighter than I am, and you invite Him to hang out with you in your life. If you have not yet, I encourage you to do so, He will bless your life more than you could ever imagine.

Over the years I have learned some pretty cool things, and I have seen some even more amazing things. Things that only through Jesus Christ could they transpire. They say, that faith is believing in things that are not seen. I can honestly say that I have never seen Jesus. Except for in an dream, hanging on a cross with two others, hanging on crosses next to Him, on top of a small hill. (The only reason this is significant to me, is because I do not remember any of my dreams except this one). Even though I have never seen Jesus on Earth, I know with an unshakable knowledge that He is The Christ, He atoned for my sins, as well as your sins, He paid the price of freedom for all of us to enjoy, if we but follow him.

I can also testify to you, that our Heavenly Father loves us so much that he sent His only begotten Son to Earth, knowing full well that the people of Earth, His children, Jesus' siblings, would kill Him. Heavenly Father did this because He knew, that this is the way it needed to be, so that we all can again live with him for eternity. But, there is a condition to that, we must accept this plan and what Christ has done for us, and follow His commandments, thereby freeing us from the bondage of evil.

The best part of this is, we do not have to do this alone. We have each other to use as support as we struggle through life. We have the Scriptures to guide us, and the best part is the Lord has given us living Prophets to guide us in these latter days.

To answer the question – "What is the secret to my success in life?" It is simple, I keep my friend Jesus Christ first in my Life! And I invite you to do the same.

So the answer to the question, **Is it working for me?** was **NO.** That is actually great news. You have realized that what you have been doing so far is not working . The thoughts you have are not taking you where you want to go. You just made the first and quite possibly the hardest choice in making a change. Now you are ready to move to the next step.

Congratulations - Turn to page   ~ 79 ~
(what benefit am I getting)

RESOURCES

www.resources.psychfit.net

THE MIRACLE QUESTION

"Imagine you go to sleep tonight and you wake tomorrow morning. During the night a miracle happened and, when you wake up, your most positive dreams for your future have come true. Remember, a miracle has occurred, so you are waking up to your life as you would ideally like it to be. At this point, you may have only quite hazy visions of your ideal future, so to help you be specific about what the real world changes would be for you, think about your answers to the following questions:

1. How do you feel when you wake?

2. What is the first thing you will do?

3. Your best friend arrives. Immediately, they notice that things have improved. What is it they will have noticed?

4. What happens next in your day?

5. Give a blow-by-blow account of the whole day of your ideal life when everything is just as you would ideally want it to be.

6. Would that be a typical day?

7. What would you be doing on the same day a week later?"

Positive affirmations

- I am successful.
- Life is filled with joy and abundance.
- Happiness flows freely from me.
- Compassion is infinite and fully surrounds me and my life.
- I am centered, peaceful, and grounded.
- Love rises from my heart in the face of difficulty.
- The love within me flows through me in every situation.
- I am powerful, confident, and capable of reaching all my dreams.
- I feel profound empathy and love for others and their own unique paths.
- I honor my own life path.
- I have always and will continue to always try my best; I honor this.
- Success is defined by my willingness to keep going.
- I walk this world with grace.
- My body is a beautiful expression of my individuality.
- I am authentic, true, and expressive.

- I have the strength to rise in the face of adversity.
- I have infinite capacity for love and affection.
- Love brings me youthfulness, energy, and rejuvenates me.
- I am a beautiful person.
- I love and treasure my body.
- I honor and respect my limitations and thank myself for the capabilities I do have.
- I trust in my ability to survive and thrive through any obstacle.
- I have come this far, and I can keep going.
- My life is founded on respect for myself and others.
- Every part of my body radiates beauty.
- I am confident in my individuality.
- I deserve love, compassion, and empathy.
- I am becoming more prosperous every day.
- I am worthy of love, peace, and joy.
- I am enough.
- I have a warm and caring heart.
- I believe in the person I dream of becoming.

✓	ABC	Prioritized Daily Task

ABOUT THE AUTHOR

Doug Wells is a psychologist, therapist, international author and speaker in the field of personal development and spiritual growth. He a Christian psychotherapist trained in clinical and counseling psychology combined with his study of Tae Kwon Do, Tai Chi and Yoga, he embraces the principles of mind, body and spirit.

Doug strongly believes in the God given gift of agency, our ability to make our own choices and choose our own path. He hopes to help get people thinking, and provide them with the tools to be able to move forward in life. He has an unshakable belief that you can change your life.

Reference page

Dyer, W., Dr. (2009). *Excuses Begone!* Hay House.

The Holy Bible, King James version, 1611 edition. (2014). Rochester, NY: Starry Night Publishing.com.

Jung, C. G. (1981). *Synchronicity an acausal connecting principle.*

Gungor, E. (2007). *There is more to the secret: An examination of Rhonda Byrnes bestselling book "The secret. "*Nashville: W Pub. Group.

Contrite Spirit (Forerunner Commentary). (n.d.). Retrieved from https://www.bibletools.org/index.cfm/fuseaction/Topical.show /RTD/cgg/ID/4612/Contrite-Spirit.htm

Porter, B. (n.d.). A Broken Heart and a Contrite Spirit - Bruce D. Porter. Retrieved from https://www.lds.org/general-conference/2007/10/a-broken-heart-and-a-contrite-spirit?lang=eng

Uchtdorf, D. (n.d.). A Yearning for Home - By President Dieter F. Uchtdorf. Retrieved from https://www.lds.org/general-conference/2017/10/a-yearning-for-home?lang=eng

Talk: Sowing and Reaping / Law of the Harvest. (n.d.). Retrieved from http://www.rogerdavies.net/talk-archive/talk-sowing-and-reaping-law-of-the-harvest

Synchronicity. (2018, June 27). Retrieved from https://en.wikipedia.org/wiki/Synchronicity

www.ingramcontent.com/pod-product-compliance
Lightning Source LLC
Chambersburg PA
CBHW021036090426
42738CB00028B/1096